Simon Armitage
Still

A Poetic Response to Photographs of the Somme Battlefield

Enitharmon Press

Still was co-commissioned by 14-18 NOW: WW1 Centenary Art Commissions,
Norfolk & Norwich Festival and Writers' Centre Norwich

This book is commissioned by 14-18 NOW and published
by Enitharmon Press in partnership with Imperial War Museums

Foreword

This new series of poems by Simon Armitage brings a fresh and haunting perspective both to the Battle of the Somme and the terrain it scarred. When we first approached Simon about taking on a commission for 14-18 NOW, we discussed the centenary of the Battle of the Somme and the rich archive of photographic and film materials held at the Imperial War Museums in London. Under the guidance of Alan Wakefield and Nigel Steel, two of IWM's leading First World War historians, Simon explored the aerial, reconnaissance and panoramic photographs that capture not just the theatre of war but the landscapes that served as its stage.

Some of these images speak explicitly of the events that took place on these eerily empty battlefields, while others are abstract, atmospheric and blurred. Each has served as a trigger for one or more of the 30 new poems contained within these pages. Simon selected particular photographs to sit with the poems, so that in effect the complete artwork is a combination of the poem and the images, each working in conjunction with the other. The result is both an exhibition, staged as part of the Norfolk & Norwich Festival, and this wonderful and original book.

Perhaps more than any other art form, the poetry of the First World War connects us to the horrors and complexities of the conflict, crystallising an experience unimaginable to those of us who now read these works at a century's remove. As Simon's poems show, even ancient, half-forgotten photographs taken for apparently mundane military purposes can inspire original modes of artistic expression, drawing out acute new perspectives on conflict, landscape and humanity. While the images are frozen at the moment in which they were taken, Simon's poems move us backwards and forwards in time through more than 2,000 years, from Virgil to the present day.

Still is part of 14-18 NOW, a five-year programme of new artworks created especially to mark the centenary of the First World War. I would like to thank Simon Armitage for creating this extraordinarily powerful work; the Imperial War Museums; our co-commissioning partners for *Still*, Norfolk & Norwich Festival and Writers' Centre Norwich; the designers David Tanguy and Sarah Krebietke and Enitharmon Press and our funders, the Heritage Lottery Fund, Arts Council England and the Department for Culture, Media & Sport.

Jenny Waldman
Director, 14-18 NOW

Introduction

The Battle of the Somme, which took place between 1 July and 18 November 1916, has become synonymous with death and suffering on an appalling and unprecedented scale. Over one million people died during the course of the campaign, with the British Army losing twenty thousand soldiers (with a further forty thousand wounded, taken prisoner or missing) on the first day alone.

Still was commissioned by 14-18 NOW: WW1 Centenary Art Commissions, Norfolk & Norwich Festival and Writers' Centre Norwich, to mark the centenary of the Battle of the Somme. My original intention had been to make a short film with an accompanying poetic commentary, based on and around the Somme River which flows to the south of the infamous battle sites. But during a period of research and through visits to the Imperial War Museums in London I became increasingly interested in the thousands upon thousands of WW1 photographs held in the IWM archive, especially aerial photographs taken for reconnaissance and strategic purposes. Aerial photography at that time was in its infancy, and often involved air-crew hanging over the side of aircraft to operate cumbersome cameras, using improvised techniques adapted from amateur photography. Some photographs were taken from balloons. The results are peculiarly disarming; the images often show landscapes prior to major offensives and bombardment, suggesting an apparently tranquil countryside, or one that conceals or betrays a darker, more disturbing picture. To my eye the photographs also have an innocence or naïvety about them, possibly because they pre-date more sterile or analytical forms of military imagery from the digital and computer era, and possibly because of their handwritten annotations, implying a human presence behind the scientific operation. Unpeopled, far less detailed than photographs taken on the ground, and less immediately emotional than those images of trench warfare with which we have become all too familiar, the vertical aerial photographs and 'obliques' (with the camera angled diagonally towards the horizon) seemed to invite additional comment, and struck me as pages and canvasses open to interpretation and collaboration. I felt the same about the astonishing panoramic photographs, taken on periscopic contraptions craning and swivelling from the relative safety of trench positions, made up of dozens of separate images stuck together with glue, some of them up to five metres long when unrolled.

I have taken, as a backbone to this project, the road that runs north-east from the town of Albert to the town of Bapaume, a distance of 12 miles. Now part of National Route D929, this unprepossessing section of modern carriageway once cut directly through the heart of the battle, and in its direction and length corresponded very closely with the advance of the British and Allied offensive and with the ground gained in five and a half months of push and resistance, of assault and counter-assault. In those terms, the road represents a yardstick and a compass-bearing and a timeline for the whole operation.

Built by the Romans and arrow-straight, the Albert-Bapaume road reminds us that WW1 wasn't by any means the first time the fields of Picardy had been the scene of invasion and conflict. The road's Roman origins kept returning me to Virgil, best known for the *Aeneid*, his epic poem of great wars and their personal consequences. But it wasn't the *Aeneid* that kept coming to mind, it was Virgil's *Georgics*, an agricultural or 'pastoral' suite of poems, consisting of four books of over five hundred lines each, whose subjects include the cultivation of vines and trees, types of soil and crops, animal husbandry and beekeeping. Scientific, pseudoscientific and at times superstitious (at least to the contemporary reader), the *Georgics* might look at first sight like a quaint shepherd's calendar or a somewhat untrustworthy farming manual. But the poetry is underscored with some of the tensions and anxieties of Virgil's own era, including military conflict, politics and nationhood, and its ultimate concern is land: the ground beneath our feet that we call our home and country, and the earth which ultimately provides our every nourishment.

These versions, from the original Latin, are excerpts from all four books of the *Georgics*. Some of the passages I homed in on felt to have a direct connection with particular photographs, others a more tangential relationship. But always at the back of my mind was an experience reported by many British Army personnel arriving in the Somme region, who saw in the rolling downs, the open heaths, the pretty meadows and the rural villages nostalgic reflections of their native country.

This book represents an enhanced, published version of the art installation *Still*, in which twelve of the enclosed photographs were enlarged to varying sizes and mounted behind transparent fascia, onto which sections of the poetry had been printed or engraved. The intention was to mimic the glass negatives of the original photographs and to allow, as far as possible, for a simultaneous 'reading' of both text and image. The poems were positioned about an inch in front of the photographic surface, to suggest an aerial detachment and perspective, to bring about a form of 'oblique' refraction, and – in a certain light – to encourage the poems to throw their word-shadows onto the landscapes below.

Simon Armitage

What turns the corn to gold; under which star,
Old friend, should the plough set out, and when
To train the curling vine to the dwarf-elm;
Sound advice for the stockman and shepherd;
How best to govern the industrious bees:
These are my themes, the songs I'll sing.

Be sure as well to let the fields lie fallow in turn;
Left dormant under the earth's crust, spent soil
Will convalesce. And as the heavens rotate,
Plant grains where bean-pods trembled and spun,
Where vetch put down roots, where astringent lupins
Colonised square miles on their fragile stalks.
But note that flax will leech all moisture, so too oats,
So too the drowsy poppy that drinks to forget.
By ringing the changes you'll save yourself hours of toil.
Revive dead, parched acres with fresh dung,
And scatter ashes on tired land.

Aerial, above Le Sars, showing walled farm, road and trench positions. The puff of white smoke is a shell burst. 10 September 1916.

Sometimes after reaping a fierce blaze is best,
Tatching the stubble till the land crackles with flames.
Perhaps the heat rekindles purpose and strength
In the soil, or perhaps the effect is to cleanse, purging
Foul elements, drawing out poison as steam.
Or maybe it opens clogged arteries in the plants' flesh,
Letting goodness pulse into new petals and leaves.
Or it cauterises, sealing broken veins
Against punishing sunlight, swamping rain
And the stabbing north wind.

Aerial 'before and after' of Pozières, 17 June / 16 July 1916.

Men of the 13th Battalion, the Royal Fusiliers, at rest on the Albert-Bapaume road following an attack on La Boisselle, 7 July 1916.

Night scene on the battlefield at La Boiselle, September 1916.

Fail to rake out every weed to the root,
Or shoo scavenging birds from the crop, or hack down
Choking undergrowth with a whetted hook,

Or pray for the slake of rain, then with green eyes
You'll watch your neighbour staking his yield sky-high,
And in desperate hunger head to the woods, shaking
Bitter acorns from the unshakable oak.

If icy downpours limit his work outdoors,
The prudent son of the soil will knuckle down to odd-jobs
He'd rush or bodge in warmer, drier months:
Hammering bluntness out of the plough's leading edge;
Chiselling water-troughs from felled tree-trunks;
Branding the herd, taking stock of provisions;
Whittling and stropping all points and blades;
Preparing willow-ties to secure the vines.
Some practise basket-weaving with supple briar shoots;
Some roast corn by the hearth or mill it between stones.
Even on high days and holidays certain chores are allowed:
Dredging and hedging, snaring and fowling,
Putting flame to wild brambles and their wicked thorns,
Dipping the flock in the cleansing stream.
Or, loading his beast, the resourceful muleteer
Might trade surplus fruit and oil in the town
For a proven whetstone or a barrel of tar.

Smashed German trenches near Ovillers, with the Albert-Bapaume road in the background, July 1916.

I'll speak now about autumn's storms...

Often I've witnessed a gang of reapers being merrily led
Into golden fields to scythe down a ripe crop.
Then the wind stirs, its battalions muster and charge,
Uprooting, laying waste to entire swathes and tracts,
Gusts out of the storm's black heart
Flinging weightless stalks to the air.
Then dark rain-columns come piling in
Drawn by legions of dark clouds charged with menace,
Barrelling forward, unleashing frenzied assaults,
Hammering the earth. Then the sky itself crashes down
So all the good work, all the gains of the season
Are swept aside. Culverts and trenches flood, local streams
Rouse from their beds and come snaking over the heath,
The sea in the background snarls and spits and seethes.
God in his fury, from his blazing fist
Lets fly his thunderbolts, and the land recoils.
Spooked creatures flee, every human soul the world over
Reels from the barrage, crouches in fear.

MARTINPUICH

TAKEN FROM E18c 8·2 Sheet 62D

KB25

Aerial oblique, looking towards Martinpuich, taken from a balloon, 21 July 1916.

Ominous, the sun – who will call him a liar to his face?

Often he warns of mutterings and surprise attacks.
War's incurable disease metastasises through the night.

A time will certainly come in these rich vales
When a ploughman slicing open the soil
Will crunch through rusting spears, or strike
A headless iron helmet with his spade,
Or stare, wordless, at the harvest of raw bones
He exhumes from the earth's unmarked grave.

Aerial oblique, above the village of Courcelette, 19 October 1916.

In this place no one can tell wrong from right;
When war stalks the world wearing its many masks
There's no honour in tilling the land, and the fields
Run to seed. Now the sickle's crescent
Is recast as a sword whose yield is death.
The East is armoured and armed, Germany marches in;
Neighbouring cities have shredded treaties of peace;
Nation meets nation in all-out attack;
The whole planet hurtles into catastrophe,
As when a chariot bolts from the starting line,
Picking up speed with every lap – suddenly there's no saying
Where it might end, no reining the clattering horses back.

Aerial oblique, Albert-Bapaume road, 16 October 1916.

I turn now to the subject of soil,
The character and qualities of different types,
Their colours and textures, what flora they bear.
First those sparse, unlovely slopes
Littered with stones and wired with thorny shrubs –

Here the olive outlives a man by a great many years.
Where wild berries decorate the hills
Or oleaster grows unprompted – take that as a sign
To plan and plant your groves.

There's one place where the spring never runs dry,
Where juicy grass, grazed all day by flock and herd
Is restored overnight by gentle dew.
By and large, soil that shows itself black and thick
When carved by the plough, and crumbles in the hand,
Is a good bed for corn.
From fields like those, slow oxen
Come lumbering home after harvest, hauling carts
Creaking and groaning under the strain of the load.
Likewise deforested land where ancient trees stood:
In need of timber and open ground the keen frontiersman
Is merciless with axe and saw,
Scattering birds to the air from their felled roosts.
Thus untamed nature is brought to harrowed earth.

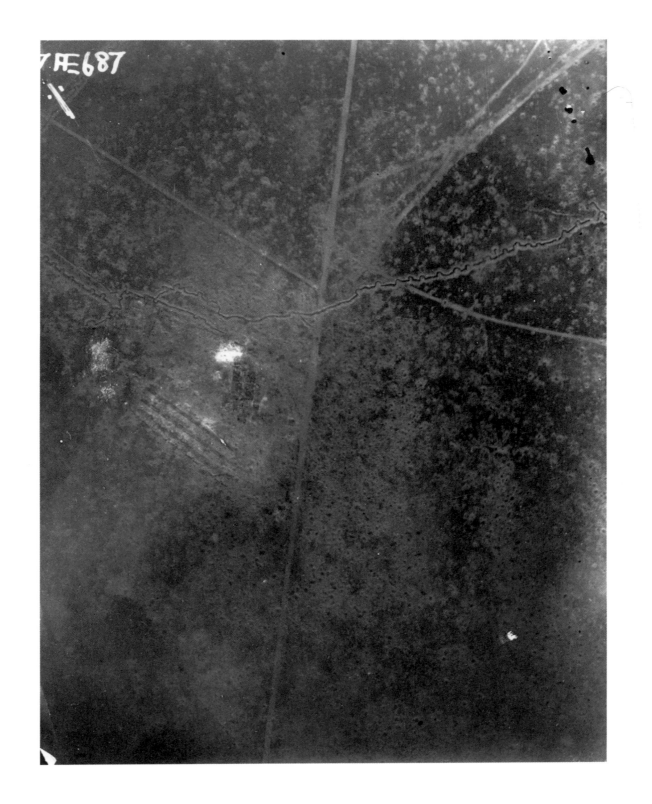

Aerial oblique, Albert-Bapaume road, 10 September 1916.

Dusty, chalky countryside is where the black viper lurks.
For hunting tasty prey or excavating their tunnels
And underground lairs, there's no better terrain.

Land that disperses noxious gases as it breathes,
And soaks up or sweats off excessive moisture,
And is cloaked year-round with lush pasture,
And harbours no salt to eat at the ironwork –
That's where the elm will uphold the vine,
Where the olive will fatten with oil. Those acres
Welcome the flock, surrender meekly to the plough's blade.

Destruction around Pozières, 20 September 1916.

34th Division attack on La Boisselle, with men in the foreground taking cover, 1 July 1916.

Clammy or swampy ground breeds fetid growth.
And save me from eager soil that's too boastful by half
And throws up a bloated, premature crop.
Use your own hands as weighing scales to tell heavy earth
From light, train your eye to earth's colour scale.
But to recognise haunted, frigid soil is a difficult art:
Bitter pines and poisonous creeping ivy
are tell-tale signs, so too the mute, funereal yew.

...terrace and trench such favourable high ground,
Stack turf to rebuff the north wind....

Crudely, to what depth should a trench be dug?
For vines, a shallow drill will do the job,
But trees should be sunk in a deeper pit
And the oak deepest of all, whose outstretched fingers
Reach for heaven and whose roots protrude
Into hell. Steadfast against raging storms,
Against lashing rain, gale force wind and lightning strike,
Impervious to the years, it stands victorious and resolute
As generations live and die and live and die
Under its broad arms, in the shade of its leaves.

Destruction near Pozières, just off the Albert-Bapaume road, 20 September 1916.

Cultivate the olive, therefore, the tree of Peace.

Under the hungry eyes of crows, scarlet berries –
Like blood-spots – stipple the forest floor.

The 'Leaning Virgin' of Notre-Dame de Brebières. Rumour had it that the war would not end until she had fallen. Undated.

Do they know what fortune they own, farmers,
Far from the scream of war and clashing sabres, living
By earth's bounty, provided for.
So what if there's no grand palace whose burnished gates
Stem a daily tide of adoring citizens, no
Loyal subjects standing awestruck at the tortoiseshell doors,
No gold-trimmed robes, no priceless bronze heads,
No vibrant dyes to colour the ram's fleece,
No exotic spice to perk up the olive oil!
Farmers exist as tranquil, honest souls, in rhythmic harmony
With the soil, easeful among calm meadows, plentiful lakes,
Shaded combes and generous fields, snoring
Under the stars, under the trees' protective boughs.

German dead in a trench near Courcelette, 15 September 1916.

It's a lucky man who fits his own face and skin,
Whose mind is tuned to the planets and stars,
Who can fence with fate and block out the sound
Of hell's echoing halls under his running feet.

Pitiful beings, our early days burn brightest
But are quickly snuffed out.

The Butte de Warlencourt (a prehistoric burial mound that became a landmark and coordinate) viewed from Le Sars, along the Albert-Bapaume road. Undated.

Loupart Wood

22.N.1682.
31.10.16 – I.

Warlencourt.

Butte de Warlencourt.

Aerial oblique of the Butte de Warlencourt, 31 October 1916.

Imagine a young man, love's ache in his marrow.

Imagine him swimming in pitch blackness, through narrows

Rocked by waves, strafed by storms, caught

In the sky's cross-hairs, under heaven's ordnance.

Sunk to their knees, two parents beg and plead,

As if life could be given back. A young woman,

Killed with grief, stands over his bloodless corpse.

The plain lying desolate, bare earth, trees without leaves.
Then in every direction as far as the eye beholds:
A stunned silence, the world shrouded in snow,
Ground frozen stone-hard to beyond a grave's depth.
A winter that feels like forever, wind off the Arctic Shield,
The sun never able to pierce or melt the gloom,
Not even when stallions haul him up to the sky's summit,
Or he bathes on the far shore setting the sea alight.
The most turbulent river is stilled and glazed
Till a convoy of wagons can set off down its glass road
And heavy carts roll by where barges once nosed upstream.
Goblets shatter, uniforms stiffen with frost;
Smashed with a pick-axe wine is handed out in chunks
And skulking fish are suspended in ice in deep lakes.
Air blurs in the flack of white flakes...

...Men burrow deeper into the earth,
Kindle what heat they can, what precious light.
In that meagre season they hunker down with board games
And decks of cards, cupping rations of grog.
Cave-dwellers, that's what they look like,
Under seven-studded Ursa Major, hounded by toothed wind,
Bodies draped in pelts, so they appear beasts.

Ruins of Pozières windmill from the Albert-Bapaume road after capture by the 2nd Australian Division, 4 August 1916.

With raw red eyes he fights to draw breath,
He gurgles with pain, his body convulses
Head to toe as he sobs. With bloody mucus
Oozing from both nostrils, his swelling tongue
Clogs his throat till he chokes.

Entire sections are wiped out, carcasses heaped up,
Putrid and maggoty, rotting above ground. Someone should
Scrape soil over what remains of the flesh.

British reinforcements moving up towards Martinpuich, September 1916.

Ruins of Pozières Church, 20 September 1916.

I sing now of honey, a taste of the heavens, nourishment
Out of the sky. Be astonished, my friend, the bees
Excel in nationhood,

each hive a state
Overseen by proud generals, with enshrined laws
For conduct during peacetime and the rules of war.

Between two monarchs bitter feuds are commonplace
And swarms are never slow to mobilise.
From miles away you'll sense them massing for battle,
You'll sense an appetite for hostilities, a violent thirst.
Cowards and dawdlers are dragooned into action.
Sounding the war-conch with droning wings
They stream into the breach, fizzing with fury,
Nerves set like wires, venomous bayonets fixed.
Back as far as their sovereign's chamber
They'll defend and engage, resolved to kill or die.
Or out of the blue yonder into the field
They'll pour from the hive, countless as rain.

Support company of Tyneside Irish going forward just after zero hour, 1 July 1916.

German POWs taken at Martinpuich, September 1916.

Advanced Dressing Station at Martinpuich, September 1916.

                                    In appearance
They vary: like lost souls tramping the wilderness
Some emerge filthy and torn, coughing up dust and dirt.
Others catch the sunlight and are gilded, bronzed.

The intense vehemence of bees surpasses
All borders, crosses every line. Riled,
They summon their poison, drive their tiny barbs
Deep into men's flesh, so their own hearts
Are ripped out in sacrifice.

Smashed German trenches at Ovillers, looking towards Albert, July 1916.

st Miraumont Road

Serre (in trees)

Cemetery

Commecourt (in trees)

Sunken road in Land

East Miraumont Road

Pigeon Wood

Puisieux (in trees)

Bois du Biez

Beauregard   Dovecote

East
(Ce

Destremont Farm
&
Eaucourt Warlencourt
behind trees

Le Sars
Village

Church

Panorama No 802 begins here.

Bapaume

Chimney
(Sugar Factory)

Butte de

Clock Tower

Church
Tower

War|lencourt

Le Barque, Thilloy
&
Ligny Thilloy
(in trees)

Bapaume - Peronne Road

Position of
Zollern Redoubt

Position of
Stuff Redoubt

Auchonvillers
(in trees)

Colincamps

Courcelette

C o u r c e l e t t e   V i l l a g e

We

Reserve
FOURTH ARMY.

The trees in the immediate foreground are those
lining the Albert-Bapaume Road.

Panorama No. 301 made on 5.10.16 from about 1000 yds E. of Courcelette

including a field of view of 130° from about W. by N. to N.E.

(Approximate Scale of Degrees (1 degree equals 1·07 inches).

mte

vvillers Road

Trees in M.t.2

Achiet-le-Grand

Trench in M3a

Bihucourt
Chateau

Bois

Loupart

Valley in
M4 a.d.

Grevillers
(in trees)

A confined space is constructed, its entrance restricted,
Its roof sealed, a slatted window opened to each wall
Facing the four winds, allowing angled light.
A bullock with two-years' growth to his horns is singled out:
He thrashes and bucks as they plug his nostrils and mouth
Then pound him with blunt blows
Till his flesh and organs are mush but the hide stays whole.
With a bed of branches under his ribs
And wild thyme and cassia pods scattered about
They shutter him in and leave him to rot.
This works best when the first west wind of the year
Musses the lake, before the meadow blushes
And the swallow moulds its igloo under the eaves.
As the season builds, a sticky essence swelters and brews
In the sweet marrow of the beast's bones,
Till suddenly an astonishment of bees burst forth,
Flightless, then agitating their wings into life,
Thirsting for dew, testing the ways of the air
Until they swarm and climb, veiling the sky
Like a summer downpour, or go bulleting past.

Panorama from Courcelette to Gueudecourt, 5 October 1916.

Photo by Paul Wolfgang Webster

Biographical Note

Simon Armitage was born in 1963 and lives in West Yorkshire. He is Professor of Poetry at the University of Sheffield and was elected Professor of Poetry at the University of Oxford in 2015. He has published over a dozen collections of poetry, including *Paper Aeroplane – Selected Poems 1989–2014*. His translations of medieval verse include the acclaimed *Sir Gawain and the Green Knight*. He is also the author of two novels and three best-selling non-fiction titles, *All Points North*, *Walking Home* and *Walking Away*. Armitage has written extensively for television, radio and the stage: he received the Ivor Novello Award for song-writing for the BAFTA-winning *Feltham Sings*, and his dramatisations of Homer's *Odyssey* and *Iliad* were both performed at Shakespeare's Globe Theatre. Simon Armitage is a Fellow of the Royal Society of Literature and in 2010 he was made CBE for services to poetry.

Acknowledgements

In preparing *Still* for publication, Enitharmon Press and Praline
would like to acknowledge the support and encouragement
of Simon Armitage; 14-18 NOW (Emma Dunton, Pak Ling Wan
and Jenny Waldman); the Imperial War Museums (Madeleine
James, Sophy Moynagh, Nigel Steel and Alan Wakefield);
Norfolk & Norwich Festival (William Galinsky and his team);
Writers' Centre Norwich (Chris Gribble, Sam Ruddock and
their team); and The Cogency (Selina Ocean and Janice White).
At Enitharmon Press my colleagues Isabel Brittain, Kathryn
McCandless and Lavinia Singer have given valuable and
cheerful assistance throughout.

Stephen Stuart-Smith
Director, Enitharmon Press

First published in May 2016
by Enitharmon Press
10 Bury Place
London WC1A 2JL

www.enitharmon.co.uk

Reprinted in August 2016

This book is commissioned by 14-18 NOW and published
by Enitharmon Press in partnership with Imperial War Museums,
Norfolk & Norwich Festival and Writers' Centre Norwich

Distributed in the UK
by Central Books
50 Freshwater Road
Chadwell Heath
London RM8 1RX

Distributed in the USA and Canada
by Independent Publishers Group
814 North Franklin Street
Chicago, IL 60610, USA
www.ipgbooks.com

ISBN 9781911253136

9 781911 253136

ISBN: 978-1-911253-13-6

Enitharmon Press gratefully acknowledges the financial
support of Arts Council England, through Grants for the Arts.

British Library Cataloguing-in-Publication Data.
A catalogue record for this book is available from the British Library.

Design by Praline: Sarah Krebietke, David Tanguy
First printed by Unicum, The Netherlands. This reprint is by Gomer Press, Wales.

Still was first exhibited at East Gallery, Norwich, in May 2016,
as part of Norfolk & Norwich Festival.

Still was co-commissioned by 14-18 NOW: WW1 Centenary Art Commissions, Norfolk & Norwich Festival and Writers' Centre Norwich

This book is commissioned by 14-18 NOW and published by Enitharmon Press in partnership with Imperial War Museums

14-18 NOW: WW1 Centenary Art Commissions is supported by the National Lottery through the Arts Council England and the Heritage Lottery Fund and by the Department for Culture Media and Sport

Supported using public funding by